Women's Fashion Adult Coloring Book
19th Century Fashion
(late 1700's to late 1800's)
25 Grayscale Images

Adult Coloring Book
GRACE BRANNIGAN

Design Elaine Warfield

IG442243

Author Website: http://www.ColoringBooksForAdults.info
Copyright 2016 Elaine Warfield
ISBN-13- 978-1523889679
ISBN-10: 1523889675

Please check out my other coloring books:
Detailed Mandala Coloring Books 1 through 4
Be My Valentine Coloring Book, Vintage Valentine Postcards:
Plus Valentines to Color, Cut and Send: 25 Grayscale Images, Adult Coloring Book
Detailed Alphabet Coloring Book: 25 Baroque Grayscale Images
Renaissance Masks: 25 Grayscale Images
On the Go Pocket Size Coloring Books
Fairies in the Garden
Scenic Catskill Mountains: 25 Photographs to Color

License Notes

∞ ∞ ∞ ∞ ∞ ∞ ∞ ∞ ∞ ∞ ∞ ∞ ∞ ∞ ∞ ∞

Please leave a review where you bought this coloring book and share your coloring images. It really helps the author and other buyers. Please check out my other coloring books and visit my website at www.ColoringBooksforAdults.Info.

Questor Books, P.O. Box 100, East Jewett, New York, 12424 USA

Meditation for your brain -- allow coloring to soothe you.

∝ ∞ ∞ ∞ ∞ ∞ ∞ ∞ ∞ ∞ ∞ ∞ ∞ ∞ ∞ ∞ ∞

How to Color Grayscale: Coloring *Grayscale* images is a fun way to explore and color and it makes shading easier to learn when you follow the shading already in the images. The end result is a uniquely rich and rewarding colored image. The cover for this book was colored using permanent markers, gel and glitter pens. Experiment, have fun!

Coloring has been shown to reduce stress and offer meditative release. Create your own visually appealing art using crayons, colored pencils, felt tip markers, ink pens, art pencils, gel pens, glitter pens. There is no limit to your creativity and genius.

Please leave a review where you bought this coloring book and share your coloring images. It really helps the author and other buyers. Please check out my other coloring books and visit my Facebook page **Coloring Books for Adults Info.**

Color to your heart's content

44

I hope you enjoyed these lovely grayscale images to color. Thank you for purchasing. Please go back to where you bought this book and leave feedback. It really helps the authors and potential buyers. Check out my website for monthly giveaways, other coloring books, journals and sketchbooks!

Facebook: Coloring Books For Adults Info

Website: http://www.ColoringBooksForAdults.info

Twitter: @ColoringAdults